HOW TO START AND MIND YOUR OWN BUSINESS SUCCESSFULLY

Step By Step Guide To Turn Passionate Ideas To Profitable Start Up

By

CHRIS BRIGHT WELL

COPYRIGHT

Copyright © 2020 by Chris Bright Well

All rights Reserved. No part of this book maybe used or reproduced in any manner whatsoever without written permission except in the case of brief quotations embodied in critical articles or reviews.

DEDICATION

To All Passionate Entrepreneurs, I Dedicate This Book To You And Hope You Find It Useful.

TABLE OF CONTENTS

COPYRIGHT	II
DEDICATION	III
BUILD THE ENTREPRENEUR IN YOU	1
DEFINE YOUR VISION	1
CHOOSING A LEGAL BUSINESS STRUCTURE	7
FILLING A NEED	12
VALIDATING YOUR BUSINESS IDEA	14
BUSINESS IDEAS RESEARCH	18
MARKETING YOUR BUSINESS	23
YOUR MARKETING PLAN	25
UNDERSTANDING TAXES	29
HIRING THE RIGHT PEOPLE	36
FINANCING YOUR BUSINESS	41

UNDERSTANDING MARKETS — 50

PERFECTLY WRITTEN BUSINESS PLAN — 58

Do Research. — 60
Determine the Purpose of Your Plan. — 61
Create a Company Profile. — 62
Have a Strategic Marketing Plan in Place. — 64

WHY WRITE A BUSINESS PLAN? — 67

BASIC BUSINESS PLAN GUIDELINES — 69

TEN WAYS TO RUIN YOUR BUSINESS PLAN — 71

BUSINESS PLAN OUTLINE — 74

SECTION ONE: THE BUSINESS — 76

SECTION TWO: — 91

FINANCIAL DATA — 91

STEPS IN FINANCIAL PROJECTIONS — 95

FIXED ASSET/START-UP EXPENSE LIST — 98

BUILD THE ENTREPRENEUR IN YOU
Define Your Vision.

There are unique qualities of successful people. They are more careful about their lives more than the average person. They monitor closely their visions and their purposes in life. One thing they do is to take the time to construct mental images that direct them to their journey. When others are winging it, they plan their life mission and business goals on paper.

They talk more often about their imagination. Start living your life this way.

Proper Time Management.

Successful Entrepreneurs manage their time very well. Many do plan their day before it begins. This is a popular activity but few persons practice it. So if you ever have a goal to start a business or pursue any worthwhile vision, manage your time.

The most valuable asset you have is your time. Value and Plan your days, weeks, months, and years.

Be Goal Oriented

Successful business owners are goal oriented. No matter what the obstacle are, they keep moving. They take the time to clearly define what it is that they wanted to do. They stopped and thought about their life, and what it was that they wanted to accomplish. This gave them the drive to see the task all the way to its outcome.

Handle Facts Purposefully

Most people make decisions from emotion and assumptions. Successful entrepreneurs base their decisions from fact-based thinking.

Since you'regoing to be your own boss. Do things differently. Check available facts and figure before drawing conclusions.

Remember that there are many entrepreneurs but few successful ones. Always strive to make accurate decisions rooted in Actual Facts.

Live To Provide Value

All Entrepreneurs know that value must be given. Giving value always lead to value

being returned.

This is the Law of Reciprocity. What you give out, you shall receive. There is nothing as something for nothing.

Constantly work to become valuable, this will attracts the personal associations that lead to greater financial success.

Change the Way You Think

Educate and build yourself. The greatest room is the room of improvement. Valuable experience must be gotten as this will enhance and lead you closer to the goals you desire. Keep acquiring greater skill sets, which in turn boost your confidence and higher self-worth.

Anyone can learn how to act like an entrepreneur, build the habits, and learn some business hacks to fearlessly create a business or start a side hustle.

Starting a business and earning passive income can be done either as a side business or per time without quitting your job.

Do not allow the fear of obstacles to destroy your entrepreneurial skills.

Failure is not final. There are many economic changes of previous and successive governments that affects the business economy, or bad ideas.

Sometimes we doubt ourselves, our surroundings, and our abilities.

Self-doubt is a major killer of dreams, long before any external factors can come into play.

CHOOSING A LEGAL BUSINESS STRUCTURE

There are several options for the legal structure of your business. A written agreement reviewed by an attorney is essential. Here's an overview:

Sole Proprietorship: In this form of doing business, one person (you) owns and operates the business. On the plus side, your business earnings are taxed just once, and you alone are in charge of all business decisions. On the downside, sole proprietors are personally liable for any claims against their businesses, and often have more trouble getting financing. Many companies start out as sole proprietorships and then switch to more complex structures.

Partnership:
In a general partnership, both partners manage the business and are responsible for their debts. In a limited partnership, individual (limited) partners are investors but do not control the business. One advantage of partnership is that:

The partnership doesn't pay tax; partners report profits or losses on their personal tax returns.

The disadvantage: Partners are personally liable for any debts of the business

Corporation (conventional):

Incorporating protects you from liability for the company's debts or claims against it. Acorporation can sell the stock, enabling you to raise money. However, corporations are strictly regulated and are taxed twice—the corporation pays income tax, and shareholders pay taxes on any dividends. When it comes to the nuts and bolts of launching your new business, there are three primary considerations:

S -corporation

An S corporation protects owners against liability and provides more tax benefits than a corporation. The corporation doesn't pay federal income taxes; profits and losses are reported on shareholders' individual tax returns. But complying with regulations can be costly and time-consuming, and you're limited to a set amount of shareholders, which maybe restrictive if you're seeking to raise lotsof capital.

Limited Liability Company (LLC):

An LLC offers liability protection like a corporation, but without double taxation, because earnings and losses are reported on the owners' personal taxes. There is no limit on the number of members. Owners or members in a multiple-member LLC should have a written membership agreement reviewed by an attorney.

Always discuss your legal options with your attorney and accountant before making a decision. Mentors are also available to help you understand your options.

GOVERNMENT REGULATIONS AND YOUR BUSINESS

To keep your new business on the right side of the law, understand the government regulations you must comply with.

All businesses need to be registered either in the state where they will be doing business (LLCs and corporations) or their county of residence (sole proprietors).

Wherever registered, the company needs a physical address (not a P.O. Box). Registration fees are usually under $500; there are also annual fees, which vary. Companies can be registered in one state as a domestic company and in other countries as a foreign company. Depending upon the nature of the business, some companies also need to obtain state, county, and/or municipal licenses. Contact your city and county for more information and discuss your legal options with your attorney.

FILLING A NEED

Define a Market Need

A good business idea fills a need that exists in themarket. You may have come up with your business idea because you, your friends, or your family saw a need for a product or service you couldn't find.May be the product or service exists, but you think
you can do it better.

Here are some questions to ask:

What need does my product or service fill?

What problem does it solve?

What are the features and benefits of my product or service? (Features are the components of your product. For instance, Bike's features might include a high-tech braking system and puncture-proof tires. The benefits of those features are safety and a smoother ride.)

What is my competitive advantage? (How is you ridea different from, or better than, the competition

What is my business model? (How will you produce, deliver and market the product or service,and how will you make money

You're reading this book because you have an idea for a business. May be you have ideas for more than one business, or perhaps you just know that you want to start a business but don't have a concrete concept in mind. Use the steps below to develop or fine-tune your business concept.

A good business idea fills a need that exists in themarket. You mayhave come upwith your businessidea because you, your friends,or your family saw a need for a product or serviceyou couldn't find.

VALIDATING YOUR BUSINESS IDEA

Get input on your business idea by giving a Mentor, friend, or family member are levator pitch (two minutes or less) explaining your business concept. Have them ask you questions and offer honest feedback.

Hearing whatsomeone else thinksof your idea will helpyou clarify yourthoughts.

Examine YourPersonal Background

If you don't yet have a firm business idea in mind, assessing your life and work experience can help you come up with one. If you do have a business idea, review your past experience to see how well it supports your concept.

CHECKLIST:

how do my skills and experience fit with my idea?

Suppose you want to open a bakery. If you have worked in food service or retailing, those kills will help you in running your new business. If you haven't, you may need to learn more about these industries and gain experience before you move forward.

How risk-tolerant am I? How does my experience affect my startup risk?

Past experience can minimize the risk of starting a business.

Many people dream of opening restaurants, but this industry has a high failure rate. If you have no restaurant experience, your risk will be even higher. Taking into account your experience and the potential risk of your startup, assess how comfortable you feel with moving forward.

How can I modify my idea to fit my experience?

If your idea seems too risky given your experience, consider an alternative. Using the example above, for instance, a person with no restaurant experience might find a lower-risk business such as catering or a cup cake shop.

Simply ask these` questions

Do I have a passion for selling this idea to others?

You need to be able to convince customers, investors, and potential partners,

BUSINESS IDEAS RESEARCH

Research Your Industry

Another way to fine-tune your business idea is by researching the industry you want to enter. You'll want to know:

Growth trends: How fast can a business in this

industry expect to grow?

Profitability: What kind of profit can you expect to make?

What are the average margins in the industry?

Trends:

What current and future trends like (demographic, economic, global) are affecting the industry?

Life cycle:

The chart below illustrates the concept of the lifecycle. Ideally, you want to choose an industry that's either at an early stage in its life cycle or in the reinvention stage. Selecting an industry in the mature or declining steps makes it harder to compete.

Consider Your Target Market

Who will your business serve? You can't be all things to all people. To create a winning concept, you need to narrow your market focus. Ask yourself these questions:

Channel position:

Where in the sales chain will your customers fall? In other words, are you selling to retailers, wholesalers, consumers, or other businesses?

Number:

How big is your potential market?

Income level/ability to pay:

Are your Customers upscale or bargain hunters?

Demographics:

What are the demographic characteristics of your market (location, company size, sex, age, marital status, and education level)?

Lifestyle:

Are your target customers urban or rural? How do they spend their work, leisure, and personal time?

Habits:

What are the spending habits of your target market?

ADJUST YOUR PRICE AS NEEDED:

Monitor customer demand. Is your product orservice selling? If not, rethink your pricing. Compare your sales to the competition.Are your sales similar to, better than or worse than theirs? Ensure you're providing value commensurate with your price. Consider using credit terms or bundling products/services to make your offerings more attractive. Before increasing prices, look for ways to reduce your costs.

Marketing Your Business

To create your brand, begin by thinking about what you want your business to be known for. Do you want to be the low-price leader?

The Premium luxury product? The company with the fastest service? The company with the friendliest employees?

Next, fill out the Product and Service Description Worksheet on the next page. List anything that makes your products or services stand out from the competition, including:

Special benefits

(How your product/service fills a need or solves a problem)

Unique features

(Physical attributes of the product/service)

Limits and liabilities

(What kinds of guarantees or return policies do you offer Production and delivery methods

(One-day delivery? Hand made products

Suppliers

(Are you an authorized reseller of well-known brand Intellectual property, special permits (Is your product/service one-of-a-kindThe first step to marketing your business is creating your brand. Whatis a brand?

Simply put, it's the imageof your business—what peoplethink of when they hear yourbusiness's name. Your brand identityis crucial because all of your marketing activities will work to promote and enhance your brand, building brand recognition.

YOUR MARKETING PLAN

Here's a breakdown of what your marketing plan should include.

1) YOUR TARGET MARKET

Explain your target market, including size, spending habits, demographics, and location.

2) YOUR PRODUCT OR SERVICE

How is your product or service different from and better than the competitions? What need does it fill, or what problem does it solve?

3) WHICH MARKETINGCOMMUNICATION METHODSYOU WILL USE

Conventional marketing methods include:

Advertising: Radio, Tv, Newspaper, Magazine, Direct Mail, Yellow Pages,

Online Public relations

(Print, radio,TV, blogs)

Collateral

(Print marketing materials; business cards, brochures, stationery, flyers)

Internet

(Websites, e-mail, social networks,blogs, newsletters)

Product samples, Specialoffers

Presentation material, signage

In the same way, your business planexplains your business idea, strategy, andoperations, your marketing plan lays out you rmarketing message and how you plan to communicate.

YOUR MARKETING STRATEGY

This part of your marketing plan outlines a roadmap on how you will market your business throughout the year. Include:

Marketing message Channel choice/sales approach (direct sales, Internet sales, etc.)

Methods used and related cost. Include one-time costs (such as a booth at a trade show, or the cost of designing your website), periodic expenses (website maintenance, monthly ads, annuallistings), how much staff time will be spent on marketing and how much that will cost, and anyother promotional activity.

Measure the effectiveness of each marketing strategy and adjust accordingly.

Different marketing methods work best for different target markets and typesof businesses. When planning the marketing mix, take into account who you are selling to and how you sell.

• Business to Business (B2B) for a product

- Business to Business (B2B) for a service
- Business to Consumer (B2C) for a product
- Business to Consumer (B2C) for a service
- Internet sales

UNDERSTANDING TAXES

Understanding your tax obligations and preparing taxes can be confusing and complicated. If returns are neglected or filed improperly, penalties and excess payments may be levied. We provide an overview to guide youon filing and paying the appropriate taxes. Consult with a tax advisor or an accountant to help you understand your obligations and/or prepare your return.

Employer Identification Number (EIN)

An **EIN** identifies the business for federal and state tax purposes. Many financial institutions will not open a commercial banking account under an assumed (doing business as – DBA) name without the **EIN**. Sole proprietorships without employees are not required to have an EIN and may use the owner's social security number for tax purposes, but a sole proprietor without employees may apply for and receive an EIN as an alternative to using a social security number. Using a social security number could increase the chances of identity theft.

An EIN must be obtained if the business pays wages to one or more employees, whether set up as a partnership, a corporation for-profit or nonprofit, a limited liability company, a trust or estate, or a sole proprietorship. NOTE: If an owner of a corporation provides services to the corporation, the owner is an employee of the corporation and subject to all employment taxes.

An EIN is required on any return, statement, or another document if you are an employer. Individuals who file Schedule C or I must use EINs when filing excise, employment, alcohol, tobacco, or fire arms returns.

Important notes:

If you become the new owner of an existing business, you cannot use the EIN of the previous owner.

An existing business that adds, opens, or acquires a new operation of a similar type may use its current EIN for both the existing and new operations. However, a new establishment must obtain its own EIN if its line of business is different from the existing operation.

An EIN form (SS-4) can be obtained from the IRS online at **www.irs.gov** or call them. The application should be completed early enough to allow processing time for an EIN number to be issued.

Personal Income Tax

As a sole proprietor or partner, the owner pays taxes on the income from the business on a personal income tax return with the state and federal governments. You will also file a new schedule that identifies the income and expenses of the business. Partners file a partnership return in addition to the personal income tax return that distributes profits and losses between the partners according to the partnership agreement. Corporations pay taxes on the business income at corporate tax rates. Shareholders and employees (including paid corporate officers) pay individual income tax on any salary and dividends received from the corporation.

Employer Taxes

Any employer of one or more persons must withhold federal, state, and possibly local income taxes from the wages paid to employees. Employers are also responsible for paying into the Social Security and Medicare systems as well as withholding a matched amount from the employee's wages. State and federal unemployment insurance payments must be paid entirely by the employer and not from an employee's wages.

Self-Employment Taxes

Just as employers must withhold tax and report it to various government agencies, so must self-employed individuals, or those working for self-employers. You are considered self-employed if you operate a trade, business, or profession, either by yourself or as a partner.

Payroll Taxes

Any business with employees of any type must comply with federal and state payroll tax requirements. This is true even if you are the sole employee of a corporation that you own. It is critical that you understand the various deadlines and conditions or that you use the services of someone who does.

Income Tax Withholding

Any employer of one or more persons must withhold federal and state income taxes from wages paid to employees. A city income tax may also apply.

Employees add another layer of complexity to your business that requires careful consideration and planning. It is essential to hire the right people, train them well, keep them happy so they will stay, and be aware of taxes and legal requirements.

HIRING THE RIGHT PEOPLE

Hiring and managing employees is complicated and expensive. It is wise to consult an accountant and attorney before hiring employees to ensure that sound record-keeping systems are in place, all the necessary paperwork is completed, and legal requirements are met. Make sure your decision to hire employees fits in with your goals as outlined in your business plan.

- Prepare a written job description that indicates precisely what is expected of each employee.
- Interview several people and select the one with the best qualifications. The majority of employers consider the attitude of potential

employees as the number one trait in their hiring decision.

- It is a good idea to have a 30- or 90-day trial period before taking someone on permanently. The wrong employee can cause a great deal of damage to your business.

Employee Versus. Contractor (Contract Labor)

Individuals may provide services to a business as either an employee or a contractor. Whatever status an individual has as an employee or contractor affects the taxes, liability, benefit costs, and many other areas of a business. The question of employee vs contractor is a very critical issue and does not have a simple answer.

There are many different tests the IRS may apply to determine whether an individual is an employee or contractor.

Improperly classifying someone as a contractor whom the IRS considers an employee can result in substantial penalties. When using contractors instead of employees for your business, you must consult with acompetent tax advisor before making a decision.

Training and Working with Employees

Training employees is critical. You want well-qualified employees who consistently and adequately represent your business, add value to your brand and image, maintain the quality you expect, and build the right customer will. A well-defined company policy handbook plus job descriptions outlining duties, responsibilities, ethical standards, and criteria for success are essential tools. To ensure consistency and quality of work performed by employees, it is highly recommended to develop and document a training plan and/or invest in your employees bysending them to specialized training. Cross-training employees in areas other than those specifically defined in their individual job descriptions can also be very beneficial in small businesses.

To keep employees motivated and involved with the business, it is vital to develop and maintain effective strategies and methods of two-way communication.

Many business owners find it beneficial to include employees in strategic, operational, and process planning; and to work together to set individual goals that contribute to achieving overall business objectives.

FINANCING YOUR BUSINESS

There are several options available for obtaining money to start a new business or expand an existing one. All businesses must plan for cash to pay start-up and/or operating expenses, including one's own salary. Most businesses begin with the owner's private capital or loans from friends and family. Some are successful in obtaining bank financing or using a government-sponsored loan program.

Grants

Some business grants are available through state and local programs, non-profit organizations, and other groups. These grants are not necessarily free money, and usually require the recipient to match funds or combine the grant with other forms of financing such as a loan. The amount of the grant money available varies with each business and each grantor.

Founders, Friends, and Family

Many times the first to invest are those who know and trust the entrepreneur – friends, family, and the entrepreneur himself. Someone that doesn't know the entrepreneur is less likely to take risks with the company unless it has achieved extremely impressive milestones. Be aware, however, that friends and family can make the entrepreneur's life difficult if they aren't sophisticated in business. Any early-stage friend or family investment has the potential to cause trouble when you raise angel or institutional capital, so be careful on how the deal is structured. It's usually best to keep it simple and put it in writing.

Crowd Funding

Crowdfunding (which includes some forms of micro-lending) is a relatively new form of financing for entrepreneurship in which contributions or loans are made by individuals or interested parties through a networked and publicly observable platform. Crowdfunding was signed into law in April 2012 through the JOBS Act, legislation that opens up the possibility of a pool of small investors while providing fewer restrictions related to securities laws that previously had been a barrier to this kind of funding.

Crowdfunding is being used in support of a wide variety of activities, including entrepreneurship, artists and journalists, for political campaigns, charitable purposes, invention development, scientific research, and more.

Various networked platforms for this type of funding can be searched out on the internet. Depending on the platform and the defined purpose and use of funds, crowdfunding monies may be provided in the form of a loan,or they may be donated funds. There are three forms of crowdfunding:

1. **Donation**: Asking a crowd to give to your project in exchange for something of value such as a CD, t-shirt, or another reward.

2. **Debt**: Asking a crowd to loan money to your business in exchange for financial return and/or interest paid

in the future.

3. **Equity**: Asking a crowd to donate to your business in exchange for an ownership share of your market.

Although this form of funding is seen as an attractive alternative for acquiring funds for entrepreneurial ideas and ventures, there are still many unresolved issues on how rules governing solicitations and securities will be applied mainly related to equity crowdfunding (selling amounts of equity to many investors), as that activity is regulatedby the Securities and Exchange Commission (SEC). Equity crowdfunding remains a complex opportunity as SEC rules governing it are still evolving.

Equity Investment

Equity investment is money invested that, unlike a loan, is not repaid to the investors in the ordinary course of business and represents an ownership stake in the business. Equity investment is best suited for high risk/high return opportunities forcompanies developing and marketing products or processes such as game-changing technologies or other high-demand items that are far superior to existing competition.

These opportunities have huge potential returns but also often carry a high cost to develop and market along with a high risk of failure to launch. To compensate for the risk, equity investors expect a substantial equity share and a return on investment often in the 6 -10 times range.

Equity is a privately held company that is not a liquid asset, so before investors buy-in, they expect to know the company's strategy to provide them with an exit to cash out their investment.

For many investors, the only acceptable exit strategy is for the business to be acquired – meaning they are expecting the entrepreneur to sell the company. Major drawbacks to equity investment are the large ownership share (control) and acquisition exit strategies.

There are various types of equity investors. It is crucial to properly prepare for and approach the right model for the company to make a strong first impression since they have many other deals from which to choose.

Angel Investors

An angel investor is anyone who wants to invest in your business, which is likely to include your family and friends. More typically, angel investors are defined as individuals with high net worth who invest their own money in emerging companies. They usually come together with informal groups to pool their funds and evaluate investment opportunities. An angel investor is usually focused on helping the business succeed rather than gaining profits. An angel investor can and should be a right partner by contributing expertise, industry contacts, and often leads on later rounds offinancing. Angel investors are likely to request a rigorous, in-depth due diligence process with the companies they invest in, and it is a crucial part of establishing the newly formed relationship.

Venture Capital

Venture capital (VC) is money from various sources held in a formally managed fund used to supply capital associated with starting or expanding companies that show the potential for an extremely high return on investment.

The fund's charter governs how the money must be invested, which makes it critical to select the appropriate VCs and adequately prepare for a presentation.

This form of raising capital is popular among new companies or ventures with a limited operating history that cannot raise funds by issuing debt. The drawback for entrepreneurs is that VC's demand a significant percentage

UNDERSTANDING MARKETS
What is Market Information?

- Through market information, one can know the prices of different commodities in the market, as well as the supply and demand situation

- The market information also includes social, technical, and even legal aspects of markets.

What is market segmentation?

- Market segmentation is the division of the market or population into sub groups with similar motivations.

- It is widely used for segmenting on geographic differences, personality differences, demographic differences, techno-graphic differences, use of product differences, psychographic differences, and gender differences.

Whatare Market Trends?

•Market trends are the upward or downward movement of a market, during a period

•Determining the market size may be more difficult if one is starting with a new innovation

•In this case, you will have to derive the figures from the number of potential customers, or customer segments

Competitors

- Competitor analysis is an assessment of the strengths and weaknesses of current and potential competitors.

- This analysis provides both an offensive and defensive strategic context to identify opportunities and threats.

- Profiling coalesces all of the relevant sources of competitor analysis into one framework in support of efficient and effective strategy formulation, implementation, monitoring and adjustment.

Consumers

- Consumer analysis helps you to identify and collect information on the target market needs, profiles, and consumer behaviors to establish market segmentation

Products

- Product research lets you understand what customers really want, allowing you to tailor your product offering to meet their needs and giving you a real competitive edge.

Used Technologies

•This analysis helps you to know which technologies are used now at the market to produce the product of your business interest

•What are the technical content of these technologies, the costs, availability, etc.?

Risks involved

- Risk analysis is a technique used to identify and assess factors that may jeopardize the success of a business

- This technique also helps to define preventive measures to reduce the probability of these factors from occurring and identify counter measures to successfully deal with these constraints when they develop to avert possible adverse effects on the competitiveness of the company

Perfectly Written Business Plan

Every business needs to have a written business plan. Whether it's to provide direction or attract investors, a business plan is vital for the success of your organization. But how do you write a business plan?

Contents of a business plan include:

- **Executive summary** -- a snapshot of your business
- **Company description** -- describes what you do
- **Market analysis** - research on your industry, market, and competitors
- **Organization and management** -- your business and management structure
- **Service or product** -- the products or services you're offering
- **Marketing and sales** -- how you'll market your business and your sales strategy
- **Funding request** -- how much money you'll need for next 3 to 5 years

- **Financial projections** -- supply information like balance sheets
- **Appendix** -- an optional section that includes résumés and permits

DoResearch.

Research and analyze your product, your market, and your objective expertise, spend twice as much time researching, evaluating and thinking as you spend actually writing the business plan.

To write the perfect plan, you must know your company, your product, your competition, and the market intimately.

In other words, it's your responsibility to know everything you can about your business and the industry that you're entering. Read everything you can about your industry and talk to your audience.

Determine the purpose of your plan.

A business plan is a written document describing the nature of the business, the sales and marketing strategy, and the financial background and containing a projected profit and loss statement. However, your business plan can serve several different purposes.

It's also a road map that provides directions so a business can plan its future and helps it avoid bumps in the road. That's important to keep in mind if you're self-funding or boot strapping your business. But, if you want to attract investors, your plan will have a different purpose, and you'll have to write a proposal that targets them so it will have to be as clear and concise as possible. When you define your project, make sure you have set these goals personally as well.

Create a company profile.

Your company profile includes the history of your organization, what products or services you offer, your target market and audience, your resources, how you're going to solve a problem, and what makes your business unique.

Company profiles are often found on the company's official website and are used to attract possible customers and talent. However, your profile can be used to describe your company in your business plan. It's not only an essential component of your business plan; it's also one of the first written parts of the plan.

Having your profile in place makes this step a whole lot easier to compose.

Document all Aspects of Your Business.

Investors want to make sure that your business is going to make them money. Because of this expectation, investors want to know everything about your business. To help with this process, document everything from your expenses, cash flow,and industry projections. Also, don't forget seemingly minor details like your location strategy and licensing agreements.

Have a Strategic Marketing Plan in Place.

Make it adaptable based on your audience.

The potential readers of a business plan are many, ranging from bankers and venture capitalists to employees, although this is a diverse group, it is a finite one. And each type of reader does have specific typical interests. If you know these interests up-front, you can be sure to take them into account when preparing a plan for that particular audience.

For example, bankers will be more interested in balance sheets and cash-flow statements, while venture capitalists will be looking at the underlying business concept and your management team. The manager on your side, however, will be using the plan to remind themselves of objectives.

Because of this, make sure that your plan can be modified depending on the audience reading your plan. However, keep these alterations limited from one plan to another. This means that when sharing financial projections, you should keep that data the same across the board.

Explain Why you Care.

Whether you're sharing your plan with an investor, customer,or team member, your project needs to show that you're passionate and dedicated, and you actually care about your business and the plan. You could discuss the mistakes that you've learned, list the problems that you're hoping to solve, describe your values, and establish what makes you stand out from the competition.

By explaining why you care about your business, you create an emotional connection with others so that they'll support your organization going forward.

Why Write a Business Plan?

A Business Plan helps you evaluate the **feasibility** of a new business idea in an objective, critical, and unemotional way.

- Marketing – Is there a market? How much can you sell?
- Management – Does the management team have the skill?
- Financial – Can the business make a profit?

It provides an **operating plan** to assist you in running the
business and improves your probability of success.

- Identify opportunities and avoid mistakes
- Develop production, administrative, and marketing plans
- Create budgets and projections to show financial outcomes

It **communicates your idea** to others, serves as a selling tool, and provides the basis for your financing proposal.

- Determine the amount and type of financing needed

- Forecast profitability and investor return on investment
- Forecast cash flow, show liquidity and ability to repay debt

Who will use the plan? If you don't use the plan to raise money, your plan will be internal and maybe less formal. If you are

Presenting it to outsiders as a financing proposal, presentation quality and thorough financial analysis iscritical.

Basic Business Plan Guidelines

Writing a Business Plan will probably take a lot of time. Up to 100 hours or more is not uncommon for a new business that requires a lot of research.

A typical plan will have **three sections**. Section one is a written section
Describing the Management and Marketing aspects of the business. Section Two includes financial projections. Section Three is supplemental information. A short (3-5 pages) **Executive Summary** is often added at the beginning of more complex business plans.

• **Section One** should be thorough but concise and to-the-point. Use headlines, graphs, and bullets to improve readability. The length of this

section is usually 10 - 20 pages.

• **Section Two** describes in numbers the outcome of your business

strategies and plans. Your financial projections should be based on facts

and research, not wild guesses. Be prepared to justify your numbers.

• **Section Three** contains supporting information to reinforce the first two sections. This section's contents will vary with your type of business.

Owners should be very involved in the planning process. Hiring someone to do it or delegating it to someone who is not a vital member of the company will result in an inferior plan. No plan (or a reduced plan) is a leading cause of business failure. You can improve your chances of success with a good Business Plan.

Ten Ways to Ruin Your Business Plan

These errors in business plan preparation and presentation will undermine the credibility of the plan and hurt your chances to receive funding:

• **Submitting a rough copy** (with coffee stains and typos) tells the reader that management doesn't take the planning process seriously.

• **Outdated historical financial information** or unrealistic industry comparisons will leave doubts about the entrepreneur's planning abilities.

• **Unsubstantiated assumptions** can hurt a business plan; the business owner must be prepared to explain the why of every point in the plan.

- **Too much blue sky** - a failure to consider prospective pitfalls - will lead the reader to conclude that the idea is not realistic.
- **A lack of understanding of financial information.** Even if someone else prepares the projections, the owner must be able to explain them.
- **Lack of specific, detailed strategies.** A plan that includes only general statements of strategy (We will provide world-class service *and* the lowest possible price.) without essential details will be dismissed as fluff.

Especially important if the business plan is prepared for a lender:
- **No indication that the owner has anything at stake.** The lender expects the entrepreneur to have some equity capital invested in the business.
- **Unwillingness to personally guarantee any loans.** If the business owner isn't willing to stand behind his or her company, then why should the bank?

- **Starting the plan with unrealistic loan amounts or terms.** Do your home work and propose a realistic structure.

- **Too much focus on collateral.** Even for a cash-secured loan, the banker is looking toward projected profits for repayment of the loan. Cash flow should be emphasized as the source of repayment

Business Plan Outline

Cover Sheet: Business Name, Address, Phone Number, Principals

Executive Summary or Statement of Purpose

Table of Contents

Section One: The Business

A. Description of Business

B. Products/Services

C. Market Analysis

D. Marketing Plan

E. Location

F. Competition

G. Management and Operations

H. Personnel

I. Application and Effect of Loan or Investment

Section Two: Financial Data

A. Projected Financial Statements

Income Statements

Cash Flow Statements

Balance Sheets

Assumptions to Projected Financial Statements

B. Break-Even Analysis

C. Sources and Uses of Funds

Section Three: Supporting Documents, Historical financial statements, tax returns, resumes, reference letters, personal financial statements, facilities diagrams, letters of intent, purchase orders, contracts, etc.

Section One: The Business

The following pages describe in detail each part (A through I) of the previous Business Plan Outline. Disregard any questions that do not apply to your business.

A. Description of the Business

Part A provides an overview of crucial information that is developed in greater detail in the following pages. **Aim for clarity and simplicity** in this part. Too much detail here gets in the way of the main ideas. **The**

Elevator Test - Can you explain your basic business idea in the time it takes to get from the lobby to the 5th floor?

Basic Questions:

1) What general type of business is this?

2) What is the status of the business? Start-up, expansion, or take-over?

3) What is the business form? Sole Proprietorship, Partnership, Corporation, or Limited Liability Company?

4) What are your products?

5) Who are (will be) your customers?

Additional Questions for Start-Ups:

1) Why will **you** be successful in this business?

2) What is your experience with this type of business?

3) What will be special or unique about this business?

4) Why will your business be successful?

Additional Questions for Purchase of Existing Business:

1) When and by whom was the business founded?

2) Why is the owner selling?

3) How was the purchase price determined?

4) What are the current financial conditions and trends?

5) How will your management make the business more profitable?

B. Products/Services

In this section, describe your product offering. This will include details of product features and an overview of unique technology or processes. But don't stop there and don't focus too much on technology. You must also describe the product benefits and why customers will want to buy them. For most businesses, the **products/services are not totally unique.** If yours are, take advantage of this while you can and plan for the competitive battles that will come. If your products/services are not unique, you must find a way to **position** your products/services in the mind of your customers and to **differentiate** them from the competition. Positioning is the process of establishing your image with prospects or customers. (Examples include: highest quality, lowest price, more extensive selection, Best customer service, faster delivery, etc.)

Basic Questions:

1) What products/services are you (will you be) selling?

2) What are the features and benefits of what you sell?

3) What Position do you have (or want to have) in the market?

4) How do your products/services differ from the competition?

5) What makes your products unique and desirable?

6) Why do (will) customers buy from you?

C. Market Analysis

For start-ups or existing businesses, market analysis isvital as the basis for the marketing plan and to help justify the sales forecast. Existing businesses will rely heavily on past performance as an indicator of the future. Start-ups have a more significant challenge -

they will rely more on market research using libraries, trade associations,

Government statistics, surveys, competitor observation, etc. In all cases, make sure your market analysis is relevant to establishing the viability of the business and the reasonableness of the sales forecast.

Questions for Existing Businesses:

1) Who are your current customers? (List largest customers or categories.)

2) What do they buy from you?

3) Why do they buy from you? (Quality, Price, Reputation, etc.

Basic Questions:

1) Who are the purchasers of your products or type of products? (Geographic, Demographic and Psychographic characteristics)

2) What is the size of the market? Is it growing?

3) What is (will be) your share? How will your share change over time?

4) What is the industry outlook?

5) Are there segments of users who are under-served by competition?

6) Do any of these under-served segments present opportunities?

D. Marketing Plan

In this section, you include the highlights or your detailed marketing plan. The necessarycomponents of a Marketing Plan are:

· What are you selling? (What benefits do you provide and what position or image do you have

· Who wants the things you sell? (Identify Target Markets)

· How will you reach your Target Markets and motivate them to buy?

(Develop Product, Price, and Promotional Strategies)

Product Strategies

1) How will products be packaged?

2) How broad will your product line be?

3) What new products will you introduce?

4) What Position or Image will you try to develop or reinforce?

Pricing Strategies

1) What will be your pricing strategies? (For example Premium, Everyday Low Price, Frequent Sale Prices, Meet Competitor Price, etc.)

2) How will you compare with the competition, and how will they respond?

3) Why will customers pay your price?

4) What will be your credit policies?

5) Is there anything about your business which insulates you from price competition?

6) Can you add value and compete on issues other than price?

Promotional Strategies

1) Who are your Target Markets?

2) How will you reach your Target Markets? (What Media will you use

3) How will you motivate them to buy? (What Message will you stress

4) What is the cost and timetable for the implementation of the marketing plan?

E. Location

Locations with higher customer traffic usually cost more to buy or rent, but they require less spending on advertising to attract customers. This is especially true of retail businesses where traffic count and accessibility are critical.

Basic Questions:

1) What is the business address?

2) Is it owned or leased? If leased, what are the terms?

3) Are renovations or modifications needed, and what are the costs?

4) Describe the property and the surrounding area.

5) Why is this a good location for your business?

For Mail Order, Telemarketing, Manufacturing, Consulting, or other companies where the customer does not purchase while physically at the business address, less location detail is needed. Modify the location section to fit your situation. In some cases, an excellent location may be one close to suppliers, transportation hubs, or a complementary business that will also attract your Target Market.

F. Competition

Who is your competition? Is one of the first questions a banker or investor will ask.

Business by nature is competitive, and few companies are completely new. If there are no competitors, be careful; there may be no market for your products.

Expand your concept of competition. If you plan to open the first roller skating rink in town, your competition includes movie theaters, malls, bowling alleys, etc.

Basic Questions:

1) Who are (will be) your largest competitors? List them.

2) How will your operation be better (and worse) than your competitors?

3) How are competitors doing? What are their sales and profits?

4) (If Start-Up) How will competition respond to your market entry?

G. Management and Operations

Because management problems are the leading cause of business failures, it is important to discuss management qualifications and structure. Resumes of Principals should be included in supporting data. If your business will have few employees and rely heavily on outside professionals, list these key people and their qualifications. If you are seeking financing, include personal financial statements for all principals in supporting the data section.

Basic Questions:

1) What is the business management experience of the management team?

2) What are the functional areas of the business?

3) Who will be responsible for each functional area?

4) Who reports to whom?

5) What will salaries be?

6) What management resources outside the company are available?

7) How will your products/services be produced? (Describe manufacturing processes, proprietary technology, and key supplier relationships.)

H. Personnel

The success of many companies depends on their ability to recruit, train, and retain quality employees. The amount of emphasis in your plan will depend on the number and type of employees required.

Basic Questions:

1) What are the personnel needs now? In the future?

2) What skills must they have? What training will you provide?

3) Are the people you need available?

4) What is their compensation? What fringe benefits will be provided?

I. Application and Effect of Loan or Investment

This section is vital whether you are seeking a loan, outside investment (equity), or investing your own money. It may be necessary to complete Section Two, Financial Data, before completing this part.

Basic Questions:

1) What is the total investment required?

2) How will the loan or investment be used?

3) How will the loan or investment make the business more profitable?

4) When will the loan be repaid?

5) If you are seeking equity (selling part of the business to an investor): -What percent of the company are you willing to give up?

- What rate of return is possible for the investor? (Note: If your business plan is presented to private investors, seek legal counsel to be sure you are in compliance with securities laws.)

Section Two:

Financial Data

A. Projected Financial Statements

The primary purposes of financial projections are:

- Establish the profit potential of the business, given reasonable assumptions
- Determine how much capital the company needs and how it will be used

- Demonstrate the business can generate the cash to operate and re-pay loans. It is usually helpful, but not necessary, to complete at least a rough draft of Section One (the written section) before attempting the financial section. In the written section, you will develop and describe your strategies for the business. In the financial section, you will estimate the financial impact of those strategies by developing projected Income Statements, Balance Sheets, and Cash Flow Statements. It is usually recommended that these projected statements beevery month for at least the first twelve months or until the business is profitable and stable. Activity displayed beyond the monthly detail may be in summary form (such as quarterly or annually.) The forecast period for most business plans is two to four years.

Before you start developing projected financial statements, gather the suggested information on the following pages. A personal computer is an excellent tool for financial projections, and those with a good background in accounting and individualcomputer spreadsheets may want to create their own financial forecast model.

(There are also some specialized software programs which have basic templates to help with your financial forecast.)

The quality of your projection depends on the accuracy of the assumptions.

(Garbage in - Garbage out.)

Existing businesses will rely heavily on past financial results as the basis for their forecasts. Start-ups have greater challenges. They must do extensive research to prove the reasonableness of their numbers. Examples of sources include:

Industry data from public sources and trade associations, personal interviews with potential customers and people in the business, competitive observation, and analysis, etc.

Steps in Financial Projections

For items 1 and 2, use the following Fixed Asset/Start-up Expense List.

1) Estimate fixed asset requirements for the first year. Include Land, Buildings, Leasehold Improvements, Equipment, and Vehicles.

2) Estimate any start-up or one-time expenses. Include any costs needed to begin

operation, such as legal fees, licenses, and initial marketing costs.

For item 3, use the following Unit Selling Price and Cost Analysis sheet.

3) Define each unit of your product or service and estimate the selling price and direct cost per unit. In the appropriate places on the form, estimate the Cost of Sales and calculate Gross Profit as a percentage of the selling price.

For items 4 through 6, use the following Projected Income Statement.

4) Estimate sales by month for at least one year. (Unit sales price times the number of units.) Consider how start-up, marketing, and seasonal factors affect sales.

5) Estimate monthly Cost of Sales and Gross Profit based on the percentages of sales calculated in #3 above. Use a weighted average if multiple product lines.

6) Estimate and itemize fixed expenses by month for at least one year. Include things like rent, insurance, utilities, salaries, marketing, legal/accounting, etc. Determine all categories which apply to your business but don't include expenses here that is in the cost of goods (services) sold.

Research items 7 through 10, and provide a short narrative.

7) Describe the amount of inventory (if any) required to support the sales forecast.

Express in a number of days sales or turnover if possible.

8) Describe your credit, sales, and collections policies. If you will make sales on credit, estimate the number of days after the sale before the average customer pays.

9) Describe how fast you must pay your vendors for any items you will purchase.

10) Also: - Estimate obligations for Income Taxes.- Businesses already in operation will need the latest Balance Sheet.

Fixed Asset/Start-up Expense List

Fixed Asset Description: Cost:

Land/Building _____

Equipment　　　　　　　　and/or　　　　　　　Vehicles

_____

Leasehold   Improvements
_____

(Other)_____
_____
_____
_____
_____
_____

Start-up Expense Description:

Legal/Organization   Costs
_____

Initial   Marketing   &   Promotion
_____

Licenses   and   Permits
_____

Beginning   Inventory

(Other) _____

_____

_____

_____

_____

_____

_____

Total Fixed Asset and Start-up Expenses:

_____

Note: List major items individually. You may group other, smaller items (like office equipment)
into a single line item.

Unit Selling Price and Cost Analysis

(Make additional copies of this sheet if necessary.)

Product or Service #1:

_____

A. Selling Price: _____

less

Direct Costs:

Materials _____

Labor _____

Sub-contractors _____

(Other)_____ _____

_____ _____

_____ _____
_____ _____

B. Total Cost per Unit _____

C. Unit Gross Profit (A minus B) _____

D. Gross Profit % (C divided by A) _____

Product or Service: #2:

_____

—

A. Selling Price: _____

less

Direct Costs:

Materials _____

Labor _____

Sub-contractors _____

(Other)_____ _____

_____ _____
_____ _____
_____ _____

B. Total Cost per Unit _____

C. Unit Gross Profit (A minus B) _____

D. Gross Profit % (C divided by A) _____

17

Projected Income Statement

For the 12 Months Beginning _____

A. (Cont.) Optional Method to Calculate Needed Capital

Many businesses can get a reasonable picture of their financial future by using the following
formula. If the business starts making sales very soon after opening, you may decide to multiply
monthly fixed expenses by a number smaller than six.

Total Required Capital =

Six Months of Fixed Expenses + Asset Purchases + Start-up Expenses

Column 1 Column 2

Monthly Fixed Expenses

Salaries (include owner) _____

Payroll Taxes at 12% _____

Rent _____

Marketing and Advertising _____

Supplies _____

Telephone & Utilities _____

Insurance _____

Maintenance _____

Legal and Accounting _____

Miscellaneous _____

(Other)_____ _____

Monthly Fixed Expense Sub-total _____ x 6 = _____

Asset Purchases

Purchase of Land and Building _____

Decorating and Remodeling _____

Fixtures and Equipment (plus installation) _____

Deposits on Rental Property and Utilities _____

Beginning Inventory _____

Asset Purchase Sub-Total _____

Start-up Expense You Pay Once

Legal and Accounting Organization Costs _____

Licenses and Permits _____

Initial Advertising and Promotion _____

(Other)_____ _____

Start-up Expense Sub-total _____

Total Estimated Cash Needed to Start (Add Column 2)

_____

B. Break-Even Analysis

Break-even (B/E) analysis is a simple but very effective financial feasibility test. B/E is used to findthe number of sales necessary to pay all fixed costs (and have zero income.) In your business plan, itrepresents a minimum acceptable performance.

Follow these steps to calculate:

1) Determine Contribution Margin Percent.

Contribution Margin (CM) equals Sales minusVariable

Expenses. CM% equals CM dollars divided by Sales. Note: The biggest variable expense is usually Cost of Goods Sold (CGS), which is the direct material and labor necessary to make a product or service ready for sale.

2) **List and total all Fixed Expenses for a specific period (usually one month.)** Fixed expenses do not rise or fall with sales volume. Examples: rent, insurance, utilities, etc.

3) **Break-Even Sales is Fixed Expenses divided by Contribution Margin %.** (See Example)

Example:

Unit sales price: $10 Monthly Fixed Expenses: Rent 2,000 *less* Cost of Goods Sold: Utilities 1,000 Material & Labor 3 Salary 3,000 *less* Other Variable Exp: Other 4,000 Commissions 1

Total Fixed Exp. $10,000

Unit Contribution Margin = $6

($10 - $3 - $1)

CM % ($6 ÷ $10) = 60%

B/E = Fixed Expense ÷ CM %

B/E = $10,000 ÷ .6

Monthly B/E Sales = $16,667

C. Sources and Uses of Funds

The Sources and Uses of Funds is a statement of how much money you need (and where it will
come from) and how that money will be used. This statement should be included in your business
plan is being presented to a lender or investor. By definition, sources must equal uses. The
following is an example of a typical format.

Sources:

Term Loan _____

Line of Credit _____

Personal Equity _____

Outside Equity _____

Other _____

Total Sources _____

Uses:

Purchase Building _____

Purchase Equipment _____

Renovations _____

Inventory _____

Working Capital _____

Cash Reserve _____

Other _____

Total Uses: _____

www.ingramcontent.com/pod-product-compliance
Lightning Source LLC
Chambersburg PA
CBHW070253220526
45465CB00004B/1603